The MEGA
Joke Book
for Kids

The MEGA Joke Book for Kids

Compiled by
Kate Browning

With cartoons by
Lucy Jordan

Michael O'Mara Books Ltd

First published in Great Britain in 1997 by
Michael O'Mara Books Limited
9 Lion Yard
Tremadoc Road
London SW4 7NQ

A CIP catalogue record for this book is available
from the British Library

ISBN 1-85479-256-3 (hardback)
ISBN 1-85479-249-0 (paperback)

Designed by Mick Keates
Typeset by Concise Artisans

3 5 7 9 10 8 6 4

Printed and bound in Finland by WSOY

Contents

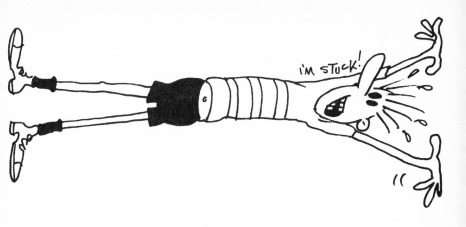

Doctor, doctor...

**Doctor, doctor, I keep thinking
I'm getting smaller.**
Well, you'll just have to be
a little patient.

1

Doctor, doctor, I keep thinking I'm a fruitcake.
What's got into you?
Oh, you know, flour, butter, raisins . . .
all the usual ingredients.

Doctor, doctor, I keep thinking I'm a goat.
How long have you felt like this?
Since I was a kid.

Doctor, doctor, can you give me
anything for wind?
Certainly, here's a kite.

Doctor, doctor, I keep thinking I'm
a pair of curtains.
Oh, pull yourself together.

Doctor, doctor, I've got a terrible problem,
can you help me out?
Certainly, which way did you come in.

Doctor, doctor, I can't get to sleep at night.
Lie on top of the wardrobe and you'll
soon drop off.

Doctor, doctor, please come quickly. My child's just swallowed my pen.

I'll come right away. How are you managing in the meantime?

I'm using a pencil.

I've not felt well since I had some beans yesterday.

Did they look all right when you opened the tin?

Oh! Was I meant to open the tin?

Doctor, doctor, I've got carrots growing
out of my ears!
How did that happen?
I don't know, I planted onions.

Doctor, doctor, I feel like an onion.
Well, you really are in a pickle, aren't you?

Doctor, doctor, everyone keeps ignoring me.
Next!

Doctor, doctor, I think I'm a frog.

Well in that case I suggest you go
to the croakroom.

**Doctor: You've burnt both your ears!
How on earth did that happen?**

Patient: I was ironing when
the telephone rang.

Doctor: But how did you burn both of them?

Patient: Well, as soon as I put the phone
down, it rang again.

Doctor, doctor, I've got jelly in one ear and custard in the other.
Don't worry, you're just a trifle deaf.

Doctor, doctor, I think I'm invisible.
Who said that?

Doctor, doctor, my hair keeps falling out.
Can you give me something to keep it in?
How about this plastic bag?

Doctor, doctor, I think I'm turning into a cuddly teddy bear.

When did you first notice this complaint?

When I stopped being a flopsy wopsy bunny.

Doctor, doctor, I've swallowed the film from my camera.

I hope nothing develops.

Doctor, doctor, I keep thinking I'm a wigwam.
Take these pills for two weeks and if you're
not any better, come and see me again.

**Two weeks later: Doctor, doctor, I keep
thinking I'm a tepee.**
I've worked out what it is: you're too tense.

Doctor: I think you need glasses.
Patient: But I'm already wearing glasses.
Doctor: In that case I need a pair too.

Doctor, doctor, I can't help stealing things.
Please take a seat.

Doctor, doctor, my hands won't stop shaking.
Tell me, do you drink a lot?
No, I spill most of it.

Doctor, doctor, can you give me first aid?
No, I'm afraid you'll have to
wait your turn.

Doctor, doctor, I feel like a pack of cards.
Take a seat and I'll deal with you later.

Doctor, doctor, I've been beaten up.
Have you got any scars?
No, I don't smoke.

Doctor, doctor, I keep getting this stabbing pain in my eye when I drink a cup of tea.
Try taking the spoon out.

Doctor, doctor, I keep forgetting things.
When did this start happening?
When did what start happening?

Doctor, doctor, I think I'm a spoon.
Stay quiet, get lots of rest and don't stir yourself.

Doctor: I can't tell what's wrong with you.
I think it's something to do with drink.
Patient: OK, I'll come back
when you're sober.

Doctor, doctor, I keep thinking I'm a telephone.
Keep taking these pills and if you don't
get any better, give me a ring.

Doctor: When you get up in the morning,
do you have a furry tongue,
a pain in the middle of your shoulders
and feel terribly depressed?
Patient: Yes, I do.
Doctor: So do I. I wonder what it is...

Patient: Tell me, doctor, when my finger heals will I be able to play the piano?

Doctor: Of course you will.

Patient: Well that's fantastic, because I never could before.

Doctor, doctor, I keep thinking I'm getting smaller.

Well, you'll just have to be a little patient.

Doctor, doctor, I keep seeing big pink monsters with purple spots.
Have you seen a psychiatrist?
No, just big pink monsters with purple spots.

Doctor, doctor, what's the best cure for flat feet.
A foot pump.

Doctor, doctor, I feel like an apple.
Don't worry, I don't bite.

Doctor, doctor, I think I'm a dustbin.
Don't talk such rubbish.

Animal antics

Why do birds fly south in the winter?
Because it's too far to walk.

What travels at 60 m.p.h. under water?
A motor pike and side carp.

It's raining cats and dogs.
I know. I just stepped in a poodle.

How do you stop your dog from digging in the garden?
Take away his spade.

Customer: Have you got a cod's head
for the cat?

Fishmonger: Why, are you doing
a transplant?

A man went into the pub and ordered
a pints of lager for himself
and one for his pet giraffe. The giraffe
collapsed after its drink and
another man came into the pub
and said, 'What's that lyin' on the floor
there, mate?' The man replied,
'Are you stupid? That's not a lion,
it's a giraffe.'

What do you give a sick pig?
Oinkment.

What do you call a travelling flea?
An itch-hiker.

Mother kangaroo: I hate it when it rains and the kids have to play inside!

How many sheep does it take to make a sweater?
I didn't even know they could knit!

Woman: Can I have a parrot for my little girl.
Pet shop owner: I'm afraid I don't need any more little girls.

One goldfish said to the other goldfish in the bowl:
'So, how do you drive this thing?'

Why do birds fly south in winter?
Because it's too far to walk.

Did you hear about the dog that went to the flea circus?
It stole the show.

What do you get if you cross a sheep with a kangaroo?
A woolly jumper.

What do you get if you cross a parrot with a centipede?

A walkie-talkie.

One goldfish swimming in a goldfish bowl said to the other goldfish: 'Why do you keep following me around?'

Why did the bald man paint rabbits on his head?

Because from a distance they looked like hares.

What do you get if you cross a chicken with a cement-mixer?

A bricklayer.

What do you call a penguin in the desert?
Lost.

Does your dog bite?
No.
Ow! I thought you said your dog didn't bite!
He doesn't. That isn't my dog!

What is parrot food called?
Pollyfilla.

**How do you stop your dog from barking
in the hall.**
Put him in the garden.

Where do you buy cats from?
A catalogue.

Customer: Have you got any dogs going cheap?
Pet shop owner: No, I'm afraid all our
dogs go 'woof'.

What kind of tie does a pig wear?
A pigsty.

There are two cows in a field.
One was going 'baa, baa, baa'.
The other cow said:
'Why are you going: "Baa, baa, baa"?
You should be going "moo, moo, moo"
like the rest of us.'
'Oh, well,' said the other cow, 'I'm learning
a new language.'

I've been teaching my dog to beg.
Last night he came home with £5.40.

**What do you get if you cross a seagull
with a pair of wheels?**
A bi-seagull.

What goes oom, oom?
A cow walking backwards.

Where do cows go on a Saturday night?
To the moovies.

**What do you get if you cross a cow
with a sheep and a goat?**
The milky baa kid.

**What did the buffalo say when his son left for
school each morning.**
Bison.

**Which snakes are
good at maths?**
Adders.

easy
Peasy

MATHS

Do you realise your dog was barking all night.
Yes but don't worry, he managed to get
some sleep during the day.

What do you call a donkey with three legs?
A wonkey.

**What did the short-sighted hedgehog say
to the cactus?**
Is that you, Mum?

Where do you take a frog with bad eyesight?
To the hoptician.

Why don't snakes have a sense of humour?
Because you can't pull their legs.

**What do you get if you cross Donatello with
Arnold Schwarzenegger?**
Turtle recall.

My dog's a blacksmith.
What *do* you mean?
If you shout at him he makes a bolt for the door.

**What do you get if you cross a snake
with a magician?**
Abra da cobra.

**What do you get if you pour boiling water
down a rabbit hole?**
Hot cross bunnies.

Where would you find a tortoise with no legs?
Where you left it.

What do you call a cow that eats your grass?
A lawn mooer.

Have you ever hunted bear?
No, but I've been fishing in my shorts.

Why do bees hum?
Because they don't know the words.

What do you get if you cross a shark with a snowman?
Frostbite.

What is a crocodile's favourite game?
Snap.

What do you get if you sit under a cow?
A pat on the head.

How do goldfish go into business?
They start on a small scale.

Why do grizzly bears have fur coats?
Because they wouldn't look so scary
in anoraks.

Have you put the cat out?
I didn't know it was on fire.

Worried dog owner: What shall I do about my dog?
He chases everyone he sees on a bike.
Vet: Confiscate his bike.

BLUB!
BLUB!
BLUB!

Why do cows have bells?
Because their horns don't work.

What do you call a gorilla with headphones on?
Anything you like, he can't hear you.

Why do cats change their size?
Because they are let out at night and taken in in the morning.

What is a hedgehog's favourite food?
Prickled onions.

Where would you find a stupid woodworm?
In a brick.

Hey, your dog's just eaten my hat!
Don't worry, he likes hats.
But it was my best hat!
It doesn't matter, they're all the same to him.
Look, are you trying to wind me up?
What makes you say that?
Well, it's your attitude.
It wasn't my hat he chewed, it was yours!

Where do you find giant snails?
On the ends of giants' fingers.

Why did the dog tick?
It was a watch dog.

What is black and
white and noisy and
smelly?
A skunk with a
drumkit.

What animal always goes to bed with its shoes on?
A horse.

How do you stop a skunk from smelling?
Hold its nose.

What do glow-worms eat?
Light snacks.

What is a bear's favourite drink?
Coca-Koala

**What happened to the lion who ran away
with the circus?**

The police made him bring it back.

**What do you get if you cross a snake with
a government employee?**

A civil serpent.

**Which hand would you use to grab
a poisonous snake?**

Someone else's.

Why did the cat join the Red Cross?

Because she wanted to be a first-aid kit.

Chortle, chortle

Where does Tarzan buy his clothes?
At a jungle sale.

What is a specimen?
An Italian astronaut.

What's purple and hard and has four wheels.
Blackcurrant jam on a skateboard.

When is a car not a car?
When it has turned into a lay-by.

What did the astronaut see in his frying pan?
An unidentified frying object.

Why did the biscuit cry?
Because his mother had been
a wafer so long.

Why is a forest always full.
Because trees a crowd.

Why did the dinosaur cross the road?
Because chickens hadn't evolved yet.

Who would you never find in a nudist camp?
A pickpocket.

What has bread on both sides and is scared of everything?
A chicken sandwich.

What cake is dangerous?
Attila the Bun.

Why did the boy throw his clock out of the window?
To see time fly.

There was an old woman from Leeds,
Who swallowed a packet of seeds.
In less than an hour,
Her nose grew a flower,
And her hair was all covered in weeds.

**Why did the man jump from the
Empire State Building?**
Because he wanted to make a hit
on Broadway.

Customer: Have you got Jane Austen's *Pride and Prejudice*?

Bookseller: I'm not sure, when did she order it?

Who gets the sack every time he goes to work?
The postman.

How do you start a teddy bear race?
Ready, teddy, GO!

Puff Puff

**What do traffic wardens have
in their sandwiches?**
Traffic jam.

Why did the banana go out with the prune?
Because he couldn't find a date.

Did you hear about the stupid shoplifter?
He was found dead under Sainsbury's.

**Who was the first underwater spy
with a licence to kill?**
James Pond.

**If crocodile skins make a good pair
of shoes, what do banana skins make?**
Good slippers.

Who invented the first plane that couldn't fly?
The Wrong brothers.

**What lives under the sea and carries
a lot of people?**
An *octobus.*

FARES !
PLEASE.

Which sixties pop group kills all known germs?
The Bleach Boys.

There was a young man from Dungall,
Who went to a fancy dress ball.
He thought he would risk it,
And go as a biscuit,
But a dog ate him up in the hall.

What happened to the criminal contortionist?
He turned himself in.

What did one parallel line say to the other?
'It's a shame we'll never meet.'

Why couldn't the bicycle stand up?
Because it was tyred.

**What did the big chimney say to
the little chimney?**
You're too young to smoke.

Why couldn't the sailors play cards?
Because the captain was
standing on the deck.

What did the big telephone say to the little telephone?

You're too young to be engaged.

Why did Granny put rollerblades on her rocking chair?

She wanted to rock 'n' roll.

What is 300 feet high and wobbles?

The Trifle Tower.

What did the traffic light say to the car?
Don't look now, I'm changing.

Where does Tarzan buy his clothes?
At a jungle sale.

Why are policemen strong?
Because they can hold up traffic.

What do you give a sick bird?
Tweetment.

What has a bottom at the top?
A leg.

Pilot: Mayday! Mayday! Starboard engine on fire.
Ground control: State your height and position.
Pilot: I'm five foot nine and sitting in the cockpit.

What is worse than raining cats and dogs?
Hailing taxis.

What do you get if you cross a bridge with a car?
To the other side of the river.

I saw a matabubu yesterday.
What's a matabubu?
Err...nuttin' Yogi!

What's the difference between a hamburger
and a dishcloth?
I don't know.
OK, you have the dishcloth,
I'll have the hamburger.

What did the Ribena say to the tapwater?
Drop in some time,
I'd be diluted to see you.

What is big, round and silly?
A fool moon.

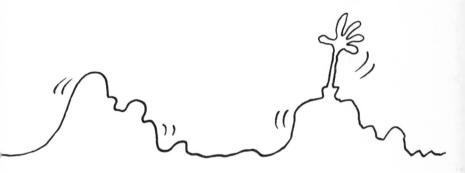

Crazy names

What do you call a woman with one leg shorter than the other?

Eileen.

What do you call a man driving a truck?
Laurie.

What do you call a girl who gambles?
Betty.

**What do you call a girl standing
between two posts?**
Annette.

Hello, Fred!

**What do you call a
man wearing tatty
clothes?**
Fred Bare.

What do you call a girl with one foot
on either side of the river?
Bridget.

What do you call a man
with a spade on his head?
Doug.

What do you call a girl
with only one trouser leg?
Jean.

What do you call a man
who's a talented painter?
Art.

What do you call a man with no arms and
legs floating out at sea?
Bob.

**What do you call a Dutchman with no arms
and legs floating out at sea?**
Clever clogs.

What do you call a camel with no humps?
A horse.

**What is green and sings rock 'n' roll
in the garden?**
Elvis Parsley

What do you call a camel with three humps?
Humphrey.

**What do you call a man with a flashing
blue light on his head?**

Nick.

**What do you call a girl
with a frog on her head?**

Lily.

What do you call a man in a plastic coat?

Mac.

What TV crimefighter was bald and wobbly?
Jelly Savalas.

**What do you call a man
with no spade on his head?**
Douglas.

**What do you call a man
with a wooden head?**
Edward.

What's green and holds up stagecoaches?
Dick Gherkin.

I'M STILL QUITE GREEN AT THIS!

**Why has Edward Woodward got four D's
in his name?**

Because otherwise he'd be Ewar Woowar.

**What do you call a woman who sets fire
to her phone bill.**

Bernadette.

Who was full of hay and conquered Mongolia?

Genghis Barn.

**What do you call a man
with a seagull on his head?**

Cliff.

What do you call a man who's always around when you need him?
Andy.

Who was Russia's most famous gardener?
Ivan Hoe.

What do you call a woman who can balance a pint on top of her head?
Beatrix

**Which Elizabethan explorer stops
wheels going round?**
Sir Francis Brake.

Which cyclist defeated the Spanish Armada?
Sir Francis Trike.

**What do you call a woman with one leg
shorter than the other?**
Eileen.

**What do you call a Chinese woman
with one leg shorter than the other?**
Irene.

Who was round and purple and ruled Russia?
Peter the Grape.

**What do you call a man
with a car on his head?**
Jack.

What do you call a lady in the distance?
Dot.

**Which famous explorer invented
the peppermint?**
Marc O'Polo.

**Which famous mystery writer was
smoky bacon flavoured?**
Agatha Crispy.

**Which famous detective writer
was white and lacy?**
Sir Arthur Conan Doily.

What do you call a man in a pile of leaves?
Russell.

What did the cannibal say when he met the famous explorer?

'Doctor Livingstone, I consume?'

What do you call a rock singer with a vegetable plot on her head?

Tina Turnip.

What do you call a boy
who gets up your nose?
Vic.

What do you call a soul singer
with biscuits on his head?
Lionel Rich Tea.

What do you call a man
with a rabbit on his head?
Warren.

What do you call an Irishman
with two panes of glass on his head?
Paddy O'Doors.

Knock, knock jokes

Knock, knock.
Who's there?
Albert.
Albert who?
Albert you'll never guess.

Knock, knock.
Who's there?
Olive.
Olive who?
Olive in this house. What are you doing here?

Knock, knock.
Who's there?
Major.
Major who?
Major answer a knock, knock joke!

Knock, knock.
Who's there?
Una.
Una who?
That's what I was going to say!

Knock, knock.
Who's there?
Yah.
Yah who?
Ride 'em cowboy!

Knock, knock.
Who's there?
Tank.
Tank who?
My pleasure!

Knock, knock.
Who's there?
Barbie.
Barbie who?
Barbie Q ready yet, I'm starving?

Knock, knock.
Who's there?
Alex.
Alex who?
Alex plain later, just let me in.

Knock, knock.
Who's there?
Luke.
Luke who.
Luke through the keyhole and you'll see.

Knock, knock.
Who's there?
Stan.
Stan who?
Stan back, I'm going to break the door down.

Knock, knock.
Who's there?
Turnip.
Turnip who?
Turnip for school tomorrow or you're expelled!

Knock, knock.
Who's there?
Sarah.
Sarah who?
Sarah doctor in the house? I don't feel so good.

Knock, knock.
Who's there?
Thistle.
Thistle who?
Thistle be the last time I knock.

Knock, knock.
Who's there?
Sigrid.
Sigrid who?
Sigrid Service, now keep quiet and do as I say.

Knock, knock.
Who's there?
May.
May who?
(sings) Maybe it's because I'm a Londoner.

Knock, knock.
Who's there?
Ivor.
Ivor who?
Ivor you let me in or I break the door down!

Knock, knock.
Who's there?
Albert.
Albert who?
Albert you'll never guess.

Knock, knock.
Who's there?
Wenceslas.
Wenceslas who?
Wenceslas bus home tonight?

Knock, knock.
Who's there?
You.
You who?
Did you call?

Knock, knock.
Who's there?
Snow.
Snow who?
Snow good asking me, I can't remember.

Knock, knock.
Who's there?
Felix.
Felix who?
Felixtremely cold, can you let me in?

Knock, knock.
Who's there?
Watson.
Watson who?
Watson TV tonight?

Knock, knock.
Who's there?
Dozen.
Dozen who?
Dozen anyone know my name?

Knock, knock.
Who's there?
Boo.
Boo who?
Don't cry, it's only me.

Knock, knock.
Who's there?
Dish.
Dish who?
It's a Sean Connery soundalike and
'Dish ish a shtick-up!'

Knock, knock.
Who's there?
Doctor.
Doctor who?
Yes, that's right. Tell me, have you seen my Tardis?

Knock, knock.
Who's there?
Liz.
Liz who?
Lizen carefully, I'm only going to say this once.

Knock, knock.
Who's there?
Hatch.
Hatch who?
Bless you.

Knock, knock.
Who's there?
Cook.
Cook who?
That's the first one I've heard this year.

Knock, knock.
Who's there?
Hugo.
Hugo who?
Hugo and answer the telephone, I'll let myself in.

Knock, knock.
Who's there?
Althea.
Althea who.
Althea later, alligator.

Knock, knock.
Who's there?
Canoe.
Canoe who?
Canoe hurry up and let me in?

Knock, knock.
Who's there?
Avenue.
Avenue who?
Avenue learnt my name yet?

Knock, knock.
Who's there?
Dismay.
Dismay who?
Dismay be the wrong door, but can you
let me in anyway.

What's so funny?

What did Red Rum's jockey say at the end of the Grand National?

Whoaa!

What did the wall say to the plug?
Socket to me, baby!

**What did the mother toaster say to her son
when he came in after midnight?**
Wire you insulate?

How do you make a bandstand?
Hide all their chairs.

Why did the man buy a black and white dog?
Because he thought the licence
would be cheaper.

**What happened to the man who was hit
on the head with a barrel of beer?**
He came to a bitter end.

What jumps from cake to cake and tastes of almonds?
Tarzipan.

AHHHHHHHHHHHH!

Did you hear the one about the magic tractor?
It turned into a field.

Why are you dancing with that jam jar?
It says 'Twist to open'.

What nuts can be found in space?
Astronuts.

Why did the sailor grab a bar of soap
when his ship was sinking?
He was hoping he'd be washed ashore.

What does the sea say to the sand?
Not much. It mostly just waves.

What is wrapped in clingfilm and lives
in a bell tower?
The lunch pack of Notre Dame.

Why do bees have sticky hair?
Because of their honey combs.

What do you call a robbery in Beijing?
A Chinese takeaway.

How do you make an apple puff?
Chase it round the garden.

What's the hardest thing about learning to ice-skate?
The ice.

Where does your sister live?
Alaska.
Don't worry, I'll ask her myself.

What did the policeman say to his stomach?
You're under a vest.

How many ears did Captain Kirk have?
Three: a left ear, a right ear
and a final frontier.

**Why shouldn't you tell jokes
when you're ice-skating?**
Because the ice might crack up.

Where does a general keep his armies?
Up his sleevies.

Why do wizards drink tea?
Because sorcerers need cuppas.

What is red and white?
Pink.

An Englishman, an Irishman and a Scotsman were all sentenced to death by firing squad. The Englishman was brought out first and the firing squad took aim, when suddenly he yelled out, 'AVALANCHE!' In the confusion that followed he escaped. Next the Scotsman thought he would try something similar and as the firing squad took aim he yelled, 'FLOOD!' And he too made his escape. Finally it was the Irishman's turn. Confident of following in his friends' footsteps, as the firing squad took aim, he yelled, 'FIRE!'

What did one eye say to the other?
There's something between us that smells.

Why did the robber have a bath?
So he could get a clean getaway.

What did Cinderella say when she took her photos to be developed?

Some day my prints will come.

Can a shoe box?

No, but a tin can.

Mum, Mum, can you see any change in me?

No, why?

I've just swallowed 25p.

What's the difference between a soldier and a fireman?

You can't dip a fireman in your boiled egg.

What did Red Rum's jockey say at the end of the Grand National?

Whoaa!

What do you call a Skoda on top of a hill?
A miracle.

What do you call a Skoda with a football in the boot?
A whistle.

Why did the baby Biro cry?
Because its mother was doing a long sentence.

Why did the man put £10 worth of petrol in his Skoda?
To double the value.

Why is it difficult to keep a secret on a cold day?
Because you can't stop your teeth from chattering.

Why didn't anyone take the bus to school?
Because it wouldn't fit through the door.

What is brown and sticky?
A stick.

What is big, hairy and flies to New York faster than the speed of sound?
King Kongcorde.

What do you call high-rise flats for pigs?
Sty scrapers.

What sort of lights did Noah's Ark have?
Floodlights.

What do you call a boomerang that
won't come back?
A stick.

Why did the cleaning lady stop work?
Because she found that
grime doesn't pay.

Two pigeons were flying over
a car dealer's yard one day and
one said, 'Why don't we put a
deposit on that Mercedes?'

Captain: We're sinking! Quick, send an SOS.
First mate: OK. How *do* you spell it?

BIG, grey elephant jokes

How does an elephant climb an oak tree?
He sits on an acorn and waits until spring.

What do you give a seasick elephant?
A very big paper bag.

What's the difference between a
sleeping elephant and
one that's awake?

With some elephants it's hard to tell.

Why do elephants live in the jungle?

Because they're too big to live in houses.

What do you get if you cross an elephant
with a biscuit?

Crumbs.

How do you get an elephant into a car?
Open the door.

When do elephants have sixteen feet?
When there are four of them.

Why do elephants wear green felt hats?
So they can walk across snooker tables without being seen.

Why did the runaway elephant
wear striped pyjamas?
He didn't want to be spotted.

**What's the difference between an elephant
and a grape?**
A grape is purple.

How do you get an elephant upstairs?
In an ele-vator.

**What's the difference between an egg
and an elephant?**
I don't know?
Well I'm not trying one of your omelettes.

What do you call a hitch-hiking elephant?
A two-ton pick-up trunk.

**What's the difference between a flea
and an elephant?**
An elephant can have fleas but a flea
can't have elephants.

**What do you get if you cross an elephant
with a kangaroo?**
Great big holes all over Australia.

**What do you get if an elephant sits on
your best friend?**
A flat mate.

What did the peanut say to the elephant?
Nothing, peanuts can't talk.

What do you get if you cross an elephant with a bag of potatoes?
Mash.

What do elephants sing at Christmas?
Jungle bells, jungle bells.

Why don't elephants like penguins.
Because they can't get the wrappers off.

What do you get if you cross an elephant with a comedian.
A big laugh.

How does an elephant climb an oak tree?
He sits on an acorn and waits until Spring.

**What happened to the elephant
who drank too much?**

He got trunk.

**What do you get if you cross an elephant
with a loaf of bread?**

A sandwich you'll never forget.

**What do you get if you cross an elephant
with Tom Cruise.**

A jumbo jet pilot.

What have elephants and peas got in common?

They're both hard to balance on the end
of your fork.

What's the best way to catch an elephant?

Dress up like a cream bun and he'll
follow you anywhere.

**What is the same size and shape
as an elephant but
weighs nothing?**

An elephant's shadow.

**Why did the elephant tie a knot
in his trunk?**

To remind himself not
to forget his hankie.

**Why did the elephant go backwards
into the telephone box?**

He wanted to reverse the charges.

What do you call an elephant in a phone box?
Stuck.

What is big, red and has a trunk?
An elephant with sunburn.

What's big, grey and lives in California?
An L.A. Phant.

What did Tarzan say when he saw the elephants
coming over the hill wearing sunglasses?
Nothing, he didn't recognise them.

What should you do if an elephant charges?
Pay the money and run for your life.

Why do elephants have big ears?
Because Noddy wouldn't pay the ransom.

What's big, grey, heavy and wears glass slippers?
Cinderellaphant.

What's grey, has four legs and a trunk?
A mouse going on holiday.

What's brown, has four legs and a trunk?
A mouse coming back from holiday.

How do you make an elephant fly?
Push him off the top of a skyscraper.

Why did the elephant wear sunglasses
on the beach?
Because he didn't want to be recognised.

Why do elephants paint their trunks red
and their ears green?
So they can hide in rhubarb patches.

What's big, heavy and grey and has sixteen wheels?
An elephant on rollerskates.

What do you call an elephant with no teeth?
Gumbo.

Where can you buy elephants?
At jumbo sales.

Two elephants wanted to go swimming.
But they couldn't because they
only had one pair of trunks.

What is big, green and wrinkled?
An unripe elephant.

How can you tell if there's an elephant
in your bed?
*There'll be an 'E' embroidered
on his pyjamas.*

Why did the elephant paint his head yellow?
To see if blondes have more fun.

What did the grape say when the elephant trod on it?
Nothing, it just let out a little wine.

**What do you do if an elephant eats
your favourite book?**
Take the words right out of its mouth.

What's the biggest, scariest movie ever made?
The Silence of the Elephants.

**What's the difference between an elephant
and a banana?**
It takes ages to peel an elephant.

Why did the elephant cross the road?
Because there aren't any chickens
in the jungle.

What is big, grey and protects you from the rain?
An umbrellaphant.

How do you make an elephant float?
Add two scoops of ice cream and
an elephant to a glass of Coke.

**What's the difference between an oak tree
and a baby elephant?**
Baby elephants have small trunks.

**What do you call an elephant that
never washes?**
A smellyphant.

**What do you call a group of elephants.
Herd of elephants?**
Don't be silly, of course I've heard
of elephants.

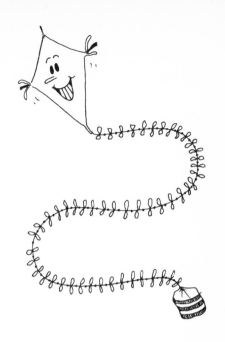

Waiter, waiter...

Waiter, waiter, what's this fly doing on my ice cream?

Learning to ski I think, sir.

Waiter, waiter, bring me something to eat and make it snappy.

How about a crocodile sandwich, sir?

Waiter, waiter, how often to you change the tablecloths in this establishment?

I don't know, sir, I've only been here six months.

Waiter, waiter, this coffee tastes of mud!

That's perfectly natural, sir, after all it was only ground this morning.

Are you the same waiter who took my order?
Yes, sir.
My goodness, you've certainly aged well.

Waiter, waiter, what's wrong with this fish?
Long time, no sea, sir.

Waiter, waiter, how did this fly get in my soup?
It probably flew, madam.

Waiter, waiter, there's a fly in my soup!
That's OK, there's enough there for both of you.

Waiter, waiter, there's a fly in my ice cream!
Let him freeze to death, sir, it'll teach him
a lesson.

Diner: What's that?
Waiter: It's a tomato surprise.
Diner: I can't see any tomatoes in it.
Waiter: I know, sir, that's the surprise.

Waiter, waiter, this soup's full of toadstools!
Yes, sir, I'm afraid there wasn't mushroom
for many other ingredients.

Waiter, waiter, there's a button on my plate!
I'm sorry, sir, it must have fallen off
the jacket potato.

Diner: Is this chicken or onion soup?
Waiter: Can't you tell by the flavour?
Diner: No.
Waiter: In that case, sir, does it make
any difference?

Waiter, waiter, this egg is bad!
Don't blame me, sir, I only laid the table.

Waiter, waiter, why have you served me
a squashed apple pie?
You said, 'Step on it, waiter, I'm in a hurry.'

Waiter, waiter, do you serve crabs
in this restaurant?
We serve anyone, sir, please take a seat.

Waiter, waiter, I don't like the flies
in this dining room!
If you point out the ones you don't like,
sir, I'll try and get rid of them for you.

Waiter, waiter, do you have frogs' legs?
No, sir, I've always walked like this.

Waiter: How did you find your steak sir?

Customer: Oh it wasn't difficult, it was just in between the potato and the salad.

Waiter, waiter, what's this fly doing in my ice cream?
Learning to ski I think, sir.

Waiter, waiter, do you have frogs' legs?
Yes, sir.
Oh good. Can you hop over the counter and fix me a cheese sandwich?

HOP TO IT! WAITER.

Waiter, waiter, how long will my sausages be?
About four inches, sir.

**First customer: The service in this restaurant
is terrible!**
Second customer: I know, but the food
is so bad I don't mind waiting for it.

Waiter, waiter, this soup tastes funny!
Then why aren't you laughing, sir?

Waiter, waiter, there's no chicken in this chicken pie!
Would you expect to find dog
in a dog biscuit, sir?

Waiter, waiter, there's a small slug in my salad!
I do apologise, sir, would you like
a bigger one?

Waiter, waiter, what's this fly doing in my soup?
It looks like backstroke to me, sir.

Waiter, waiter, I'm in a hurry – will my
pancake be long?
No, sir, it will be round.

Waiter, waiter, there's a spider in my soup.
Get me the manager!
That won't do any good, sir,
he's afraid of them too.

Waiter, waiter, there's a fly in my soup.
That's all right, sir, we won't
charge you extra.

Funny food

Why did the tomato blush?
Because he saw the salad dressing.

What kind of food does a racehorse eat?
Fast food.

What is square and green?
A lemon in disguise.

What's small and wobbly
and sits in a pram?
A jelly baby.

Why did the egg go to the jungle?
Because it was an eggsplorer.

Why did the peanut go to the police?
Because he'd been assaulted.

How do you make an artichoke?
Strangle it.

What do Eskimos eat for breakfast?
Ice Krispies.

Why are cooks cruel?
Because they beat eggs and whip cream.

Have you seen the salad bowl?
No, but I've seen the lunch box.

A woman walked up to a man
and tried to tell him that he
had a leek sticking out of each ear.
'I'm sorry,' he said, 'I can't hear you.
I've got a leek stuck in each ear.'

How do you make a sausage roll?
Push it down the hill.

What's the fastest vegetable?
A runner bean.

What do dieting cannibals eat?
Thin *people.*

What do you call two rows of vegetables?
A *dual cabbage* way.

What's white and fluffy and lives in the jungle?
A *meringue-utan.*

Why did the banana go to the doctor?
Because *it wasn't peeling very well.*

Why did the tomato blush?
Because he saw the salad dressing.

What do you call a thief who only steals meat?
A hamburglar.

What do cavemen eat for lunch?
Club sandwiches.

What's the best time to have lunch?
After breakfast and before tea.

What is small, round and giggles a lot?
A tickled onion.

What looks like half a loaf of bread?
The other half.

What do you call a mushroom who makes you laugh all day?
A fungi to be with.

What's the strongest vegetable?
A muscle sprout.

Why did the apple turnover?
Because it saw the Swiss roll.

What's yellow and goes click?
A ballpoint banana.

Laugh-a-minute

**What would you call Superman
if he lost all his powers?**

Man.

**Which dinosaur always comes first
in spelling tests?**
A Tyrannathesaurus Rex.

**Did you hear about the theft of a van
full of wigs?**
Police are combing the area.

Why was the little Egyptian girl upset.
Because her daddy was a mummy.

Do you know the joke about the bed?
No.
Nor do I, it hasn't been made yet!

**Why did the two boa constrictors
get married?**
They had a crush on each other.

What do you call a one-eyed dinosaur?
D'youthink'esaurus.

What do you call a flying policeman?
A helicopper.

Did you hear about the boy who went to bed with his pencil?
Why was that?
So he could draw the curtains.

Do you play the piano by ear?
No, I've always found it easier
to use my hands.

Why did the cowboy jump off the wagon?
Because he got stage fright.

Why did the man keep tripping over lobsters?
Because he was accident prawn.

Which vegetable is good at snooker?
A cue-cumber.

What did Hamlet say to himself when he went to Weight Watchers?
'Tubby or not tubby, fat is the question!'

How do mountains hear?
With their mountaineers.

Why did the pilot crash into the house?
Because the landing light was on.

Boy: Can I have some budgie seed please?
Pet shop owner: I didn't know you had a budgie.
Boy: I haven't. That's why I want to grow one.

What would you call Superman if he lost all his powers?
Man.

Where do fish wash?
In a river basin.

Why is the sky so high?
So birds don't bump their heads.

**'I'd like to be included in your
next edition,' said the man
on the phone to the *Guinness Book
of Records*. 'Why, what have
you done?' came the reply.
'I've completed a jigsaw in just under
a week and on the box it says
three to five years.'**

How do Eskimos dress?
As quickly as possible.

Why was the postman given the sack?
So he could carry letters in it.

**What is big, green, bad-tempered
and wears ripped clothes?**
The Incredible Sulk.

Why did the tonsils get dressed up?
Because the doctor was taking them out.

How did the detective find Quasimodo?
He followed a hunch.

How do you get rid of a boomerang?
Throw it down a one-way street.

**What do you call small rivers
that run into the Nile?**
Juveniles.

**Teacher: What do you want to be
when you grow up?**

Boy: I want to follow in my father's footsteps
and be a policeman.

**Teacher: I didn't know your father
was a policeman?**

Boy: He's not, he's a burglar.

Did you hear about the wooden car?

It wooden go.

What did the plank say to the electric drill?

You bore me.

**What roams about on your plate,
keeping law and order?**

Robochop.

Ghostly gags

What is Dracula's favourite landmark?
The Vampire State Building.

What should you do if a ghost comes in through the front door?
Run out through the back door.

What does a monster call his parents?
Dead and Mummy.

Why are vampires stupid?
Because they're suckers.

What kind of jewels do monsters wear?
Tombstones.

**What do you call
a wizard from
outer space?**
A flying sorcerer.

How does a vampire cross the ocean?
In a blood vessel.

What is a monster's favourite game?
Swallow my leader.

What do polite vampires always remember to say?
Fangs very much.

What do you call a skeleton in a kilt?
Bony Prince Charlie.

Why did the skeleton go to the party.
Because he wanted a rattling good time.

**Did you hear about the cannibal
with indigestion?**
He ate someone who disagreed with him.

Why did Frankenstein have indigestion?
He bolted his food.

What is a ghost's favourite music?
A haunting melody.

What do cannibals eat at home?
Baked beings on toast.

How do ghosts get through locked doors?
They have skeleton keys.

What do polite monsters say at meal times?
Pleased to eat you.

What do cannibals eat at parties?
Buttered host.

What medicine do ghosts take for colds?
Coffin drops.

What do ghosts eat for dinner?
Ghoulash.

Why do vampires play poker?
Because the stakes are high.

What do short-sighted ghosts wear?
Spooktacles.

What do vampires put in their fruit salad?
Necktarines and blood oranges.

How did the two vampires fall in love?
Love at first bite.

**What do you get if you cross Dracula
with a hotdog?**
A fangfurter.

Why does Dracula drink blood?
Because Diet Coke makes him burp.

What do ghosts put in their coffee?
Evaporated milk.

What do ghosts like on their roast beef?
Gravey.

What does a monster eat when he's just been to the dentist?
The dentist.

What does a postman deliver to ghosts?
Fang mail.

Why do witches fly on broomsticks?
Because vacuum cleaners are too heavy.

Where do vampires keep their savings?
In a blood bank.

**What would you get if Frankenstein trod
on Batman and Robin?**
Flatman and Ribbon.

What is Dracula's favourite pudding?
I scream.

What should you do with a green alien?
Wait until it ripens.

When do ghosts play tricks on each other?
April Ghouls' Day.

**What do you get if you cross a policeman
with a ghost?**
A police inspectre.

Why are ghosts always drunk?
Because they're too fond of spirits.

What is Dracula's favourite landmark?
The Vampire State Building.

What do you call a sorceress with no broomstick?
A witch-hiker.

**What do you call a wicked old woman
who lives on the beach?**
A sandwich.

What is a ghost's favourite football position?
Ghoulkeeper.

School side-splitters

**Teacher: Name a legendary creature
that was half man and half beast.
Pupil: Buffalo Bill.**

Teacher: When was the Iron Age?
Pupil: Before they invented drip-dry shirts?

**Teacher: What can you tell me about
the Dead Sea?**
Pupil: I didn't even know it was ill.

**Teacher: Why did cavemen paint pictures
on cave walls?**
Pupil: Because they couldn't
spell their names.

**Teacher: You should have been here
at 9 o'clock!**
Pupil: Why, what happened?

**Teacher: This homework is in your
father's writing.**
Pupil: I know, sir, I borrowed his pen.

What do music teachers give you?
Sound advice.

Teacher: Can you tell me where elephants are found?

Pupil: How could anyone lose an elephant?

Teacher: What was the Romans' most remarkable achievement?

Pupil: Learning Latin.

Teacher: If you had £5 in one pocket and £2.45 in the other, what would you have?

Pupil: Someone else's trousers on, miss.

Schoolboy: I've got to write an essay on the Houses of Parliament.

Friend: That's going to be difficult – I'm writing mine on paper.

Sports teacher: Why didn't you stop that ball?

Pupil goalkeeper: I thought that's what the net was for.

Teacher: You have your shoes on the wrong feet.

Pupil: They're the only feet I've got, sir.

What word is always spelt incorrectly?
Incorrectly.

Teacher: Can you name two days of the week beginning with the letter 'T'?
Pupil: Today and tomorrow!

Teacher: The ruler of old Russia was called the Czar and his wife was called the Czarina. What were his children called?
Pupil: Czardines?

What did the chicken study in college?
Eggonomics.

Why did the thermometer go to college?
Because he wanted to get a degree.

Teacher: In the list of English monarchs, who came after Mary?

Pupil: Her little lamb?

Pupil: Please miss, would you punish someone for something they didn't do?

Teacher: No, of course not.

Pupil: Oh good, because I haven't done my homework.

Teacher: If you had 50p in one pocket and you asked your Dad for another 50p, what would you have?

Pupil: 50p.

Teacher: You obviously don't know how to add up.

Pupil: You obviously don't know my Dad!

Teacher: What comes after 'O' in the alphabet?

Class: 'K!'

Parent: I'm worried about you being at the bottom of the class.

Child: Don't worry, mum, they teach the same things at both ends.

Teacher: I wish you'd pay a little attention!

Pupil: I'm paying as little as I can, sir.

Pupil: Sir, why do teachers get paid when we have to do all the work?

Teacher: Name a legendary creature that was half man and half beast.
Pupil: Buffalo Bill.

Teacher: You missed school yesterday, didn't you?
Pupil: No, sir, I didn't miss it at all.

Teacher: Name five animals that live in the jungle.
Pupil: A lion and . . . four giraffes.

Teacher: If I have twenty chips in one hand and ten in the other, what do I have?
Pupil: Greasy hands, miss.

Teacher: Who wrote an 'Ode to a Grecian Urn'?

Pupil: I don't know but I'd be surprised
if he got a reply.

Teacher: Does your father help you
with your homework?

Pupil: No, he gets it wrong all by himself.

Teacher: If you found some money that wasn't
yours, would you keep it?

Pupil: No, miss, I'd spend it as soon as I could.

Teacher: What happened when the wheel
was invented?

Pupil: It caused a revolution, miss.

Teacher: What's the difference between this class and a stormy sea?

Class: Dunno.

Teacher: A stormy sea only sometimes makes me sick!

Teacher: There will only be half a day of school this morning.

Class: Hooray!

Teacher: The other half will be this afternoon.

Teacher: What do you know about the Boston Tea Party?

Pupil: Nothing, I don't think I was invited.

More animal antics

What do you call a reindeer with one eye?
No idea.

What's white and furry and smells of peppermint?
A Polo Bear

What do you call a reindeer with one eye?
No idea.

What do you call a reindeer with one eye and no legs?
Still no idea.

A man was driving down a country lane
when suddenly a hare ran
into his path. He tried to swerve but
couldn't avoid hitting it.
He felt terrible and so he walked
a couple of miles to the
nearest farm to tell the farmer what
had happened. The farmer
walked back to the car with him,
saw the remains of the
squashed hare and sprayed something on it.
Two minutes later the man
couldn't believe it when the hare jumped
up and went running down the
road, turning back every now and then
to wave. 'What on earth did
you spray on that squashed hare?'
he asked the farmer. 'Hare restorer with
a permanent wave,' he replied.

What do cats read in the mornings?
Mewspapers.

What do you get if you give a chicken whisky?
Scotch eggs.

What kind of chicken lays electric eggs?
A battery hen.

**Why weren't the two butterflies allowed
to go to the ball?**
Because it was a mothball.

Two horses went into a bar and the barman said, 'Hey, fellas! What's with the long faces?'

What is a twip?
It's when a wabbit goes for a wide on a twain.

Teacher: Name one animal that lives in Lapland.
Pupil: Reindeer.
Teacher: Good. Now name another.
Pupil: Another reindeer.

What do you get if you cross a cat with a parrot?
A carrot.

How does an octopus go to war?
Well-armed.

What do you get if you cross a snake
with a Lego set?
A boa constructor.

What is a duck's favourite TV programme?
The Bill.

What is a cat's favourite TV programme?
Miami Mice.

**What is the best way to communicate
with a fish?**
Drop it a line.

What do you call a fish with no eyes?
Fsh.

Why did the fish blush?
Because the seaweed.

Why did the fish blush again?
Because it saw the bottom
of the Queen Mary.

What is a horse's favourite game?
Stable tennis.

What does a cat have for breakfast?
Mice Krispies.

**What do you get if you cross a cow
with a camel?**
Lumpy milkshake.

What's grey and goes PSHHH?
A pigeon with a puncture.

**What do you call a crab that only buys
ice cream for himself?**
Shellfish.

Has your cat ever had fleas?
No, but she's had kittens.

What is a slug?
A snail with a housing problem.

Which petrol do snails use?
Shell.

**Did you hear about the hyena who swallowed
an Oxo cube?**
He made himself a laughing stock.

How do you take a pig to hospital?
By hambulance.

What do frogs wear in the summer?
Open toad sandals.

A man was amazed to see a dog buying
meat for his owner in a
butcher's because not only did he appear
to check the quality of the meat,
but he noticed that the butcher short-changed
him and growled until he was given
the right money. Intrigued, the man followed
the dog from the shop and saw him
help an old lady across the road with her
shopping. The man then followed
the dog to his owner's house and couldn't
believe his eyes when the dog
stood up on his hind legs to ring the doorbell.
The dog's owner came to the door,
took the shopping from the dog and kicked
him into the garden. The man
watching was horrified and called out to the
owner, 'I can't believe you kicked
that amazing dog – he does your shopping,
checks your change and even helps
old ladies across the road!' 'I know,'
the owner replied, 'but that's the third time
this week he's forgotten his keys.'

When should a mouse carry an umbrella?
When it's raining cats and dogs.

What is green and hard?
A turtle with a machine gun.

Why did the butterfly?
Because it saw the milk float.

What's the difference between a weasel
and a stoat?
A weasel is weasely wecognised but a stoat
is stoatally different.

What is a horse's favourite TV programme?
Neighbours.

One cow said to another, 'Are you worried
about this mad cow disease?'
'No, why should I be? I'm a squirrel.'

What do you call a musical fish?
A piano tuna.

What has six legs, bites and talks in code?
A morse-quito.

Why did the dog keep chewing the furniture?
Because it had a suite tooth.

What would you do with a sick wasp?
Take it to waspital.

What did one flea say to the other
as they came out of the nightclub?
'Shall we walk home or take a dog?'

Why shouldn't you play poker in the jungle?
Because there are too many cheetahs.

What is brown, prickly and squirts jam?
A hedgehog eating a doughnut.

Who tell the best chicken jokes?
Comedi-hens.

What happened to the cat who
ate a ball of wool?
She had mittens.

When is the best time to buy budgies?
When they're going cheap.

Two chickens went into a bar and the
barman said, 'Sorry, lads, I'm afraid
we don't serve food in here.'

Teacher: Name two crustaceans.
Pupil: King's Crustacean and
Charing Crustacean.

**What do you get if you cross an elk
with a packet of cocoa powder?**
Chocolate moose.

**What do you get if you cross a plum
with a leopard?**
A highly dangerous purple people-eater.

How do sheep keep warm in winter?
They turn on the central bleating.

**What do you do if an elephant sits in front
of you in the cinema?**
Miss most of the film.

One cow said: 'Moo, moo, moo.'
The other cow said: 'I knew you were
going to say that!'

What is a dog's favourite food?
Anything that's on your plate.

**Why are turkeys never invited
to smart dinner parties?**
Because they always use fowl language.

Are you taking that chicken home for tea?
No, he's had his tea. Now we're going
to the cinema.